Merry Christmas

Pietro Smitth

Contents

Sam hates Christmas and everything cheery, but just a few days before Christmas his world is turned upside down...

I'M NOT DREAMING OF A WHITE CHRISTMAS

Sam knew the clock was ticking as he bent down and scrubbed the dog's wet fur. "Easy there boy," he said as the dog shook his fur, causing Sam to be wet.

The feeling was bittersweet knowing that Christmas was just a few short days away. The holiday which Sam despised, the one that left him feeling hollow.

"Sam, hurry up!" His boss Mr. Mulconey opened the door to his office and bellowed. "The owner will be waiting for you to deliver Scott! Now get a move on!" he slammed the door.

"Mr. Mulconey," Sam headed to his office. "Where exactly am I delivering this dog?"He glanced over through the corner of his eye, watching the animal.

Sam loved driving the van around. He liked sticking his head out of the window, doing the same thing the pups would do. He even loved deliveries, although he wasn't one to admit it, it made him tear up inside, when the dogs were sent home.

"On Fourth street and Main," The boss replied, "and don't be late!"

"Fourth Street and Main? But that's the Christmas Fair!"

"So?"

"I hate Christmas."

All I want for Christmas Isn't You

Brushing the snow off of his clothes, he was greeted by the warmness of the sweet shoppe. Cupping his hands around the frosty glass, his eyes studied her. In the corner, regaling an old Christmas tale to the little children, was a young woman with a cherubic face.

Pulling the door open, Sam untied the scarf that was wrapped like a bow around his neck.

Her glistening brown eyes lit up in amazement as she turned the page, the children sighing in awe. He remained in utter enchantment as the children clapped their hands.

She did a cute little bow and waved as the children scurried off to their parents. Sensing his luck, Sam picked up a menu by the counter. He glanced at it, hoping that she wouldn't notice him noticing her.

A scowl crossed her face as her eyes bore into his. His mind went blank, not having the faintest recollection of what he did to her.

"May I ask why you are scowling at me?" Sam slid the menu back into its place, not once removing his gaze.

"You, you're the one who hates Christmas and the one who knocked me over yesterday at the Market," she stated with her tone as blunt as a knife.

All twenty heads faced Sam's direction. He couldn't see them-- no, he felt their presence creep up by the hairs on his neck.

"Yeah, and?" Sam gave her a disapproving look, taking in her festive green and red holiday attire.

"Ms. Melody," a child with blonde pigtails and an adorable grin placed her tiny hands on the counter. Melody smiled as she bent down to reach the little girl's level. Only her hands were visible on the white countertops.

"Yes, Anna?"

Instantly, Melody's voice rang out like a beautiful song in his ears. It was one that he wanted to play over and over again.

"Don't hang around him. Your Christmas spirit might go away!" The little girl folded her arms giving him a mean pout.

Sam tried to stay mad, but knowing his heritage and family tree, there was no way that was happening.

She chuckled a grin, as she stroked the little girl's hair. "Is that so?"

"Yes."

An incredulous smirk crept across Melody's face, as if she wasn't entirely believing of this fact. "Okay, okay, fine. Don't you worry Anna, My Christmas Spirit will not fade, no matter what. "

"You're sure?"

"I'm positive, as positive as Santa Claus will be delivering presents this year!"

The hairs on Sam's neck stood up again as he heard that name. The name he'd tried so hard to forget.

"Fine, I believe you, Ms. Melody. As for you," Anna turned to face him, angry as ever. "Do not ruin Christmas!"

What a spirited little girl!

Sam swiveled his stool around, capturing Melody's interest. He watched as dribbles of coffee painted the white counter. "You missed a spot," He offered her a napkin.

His hand wavered as she grabbed a nearby cloth instead.

"Your name's Melody, right?"

Melody didn't acknowledge Sam's question, nor did she look in his vicinity.

He repeated the question again, this time earning a fist slamming onto the hard surface. "What do you want?"

In an instant, the sweet faced woman turned into a harsh angry elf.

"I just wanted to talk to you," Sam calmly searched her eyes wondering if they would revert back to their friendly nature.

A softness-- very subtle-- but it was there, emerged from her pupils. He steadily continued. "I saw you reading to the kids over there." Sam gazed at the spot where the kids once stood. By now the last of them had gone through the door.

"Yeah, I love reading to them," she draped a shawl over her body. For once, he noticed her silver Noel necklace, and instantly felt homesick.

"What is your special today?" he looked over her shoulder straight to the coffee maker.

Although she was hesitant, she skimmed her finger over the laminate paper, stopping a few times to tap on the pictures.

"We have French Vanilla but we're closing soon." Sam could've sworn he saw some sorrow in her face, but passed it over-- the urge to drink coffee was a tad bit stronger.

"Well that's too bad. Maybe your boss could make an exception," Sam prodded, giving her his best side.

"I'm the boss," she stated without giving him a chance to finish the sentence.

Sam's mouth nearly dropped to the floor. "But you're so young!"

A sliver of a giggle fell from her lips. "Well I'm not actually the boss. Merry, she's the owner. She's out for a convention. Besides I'm only 18."

Maybe 18 in Elf years...

Her phone rang garnering all of her attention. "Hi Merry."

Her back faced Sam, causing him to fiddle with his jacket. Likewise, she played with the felt red buttons on the hem of her shirt. "I was just closing up. Yeah, business is good today."

Her lip quivered."You're not going to be here? Why not? I can't handle the business forever!"

He watched as the panic filled her face. "But there isn't a storm."

Her eyes grew as large as saucers, and Sam searched for the source. A patch of flurries descended from the sky, causing Sam to shiver and her to groan in frustration.

"Never mind, the storm just hit," she blew in a deep breath, as she rested her elbows on the counter and put her head down.

The cubed television mounted on the wall, zapped off, capturing his attention. "Do television's normally turn off in your world?"

She was too busy continuing the conversation on her phone to notice his strange comment.

"You can't be serious?" her tone of voice hit a high note.Melody went to the back of the bakery, returning a short while later with her flashlight.

"In case the lights go out, here."Sam felt something cold and metal touch his palm. He looked down and saw the flashlight.

"What's this for?"

"You've never seen a flashlight before?" she scanned the man over.

He scoffed, obviously offended. "Of course I have. I'm just wondering why I need it."

"Because," she sat down beside him, so that their shoulders were touching. It sparked something deep inside him, a flutter of hope burned in his chest. "Merry says the storm knocked out power where she was. I just want to be prepared."

"That's pretty smart of you," Sam didn't meet her gaze, still fazed by the jolt of electricity coursing through his veins.

"Thanks," she replied hopping off the stool and returning behind the counter. "Do you still want that French Vanilla?"

Sam nodded his head and she went to work fixing the drink for him. Taking off his mittens, he couldn't help but notice her small, delicate hands as they poured sugar into the cup.

As she spun around, Sam took this time to grab a snack. Using a little bit of magic, a small burlap sac emerged out of thin air. He silently scolded himself as a yellowy powder seeped from his jacket sleeve. Using his foot, he kicked it under his bar stool hoping she hadn't seen it.

Reaching into the sac, he felt the bits of chocolate chip and instantly moaned as he took a bite.

When she whirled her head around, Sam quickly hid them behind his back.

Her eyes raked over his abrupt demeanor but Sam let her, praying that she would go back to whatever she was doing. After another glance over, she returned to stir the two drinks.

Urgency was ringing in his ears, and stomach. Grabbing a white, glass plate with crumbs on it resting on the counter, he emptied out the sac.

Setting his guard down, he spread the cookies out one by one.

Melody's voice startled him and he nearly jump out of the chair. "Where did you get those?"

She pointed an accusing finger towards the plate and then back to him.

His heart stopped, no one has ever caught him red handed before. Clutching a mouthful of cookies, one dropping, he speaks. "They were here the whole time."

His throat burned as the cinnamon spice flavour was ignited. How many times had he told his mother, "Enough with the cinnamon!"

But no, she doesn't listen, she just uses cinnamon as if it were going out of style.

"You're making a strange face," Melody said, eyeing the way Sam's lips stuck out. He pounded his chest as he coughed, causing cookie dust to fly into the her direction.

"Geez, warn a girl, will you?" she brushed off some of the crumbs that landed on her face.

"Next time when I'm dying, I'll let you know," Sam chirped out, still trying to rid his tastebuds of the cinnamon that just wouldn't quit.

"I'd appreciate that," she quipped. A thread of disdain washed across Sam's face, so he did what he was best at. Sam put up a guard--a snarky, sarcastic guard. "Here I thought you were little Miss Christmas, all joyful and stuff?"

Sam felt the iciness in his tone.

Geez. He could have passed for Jack Frost.

Seeing as she got a good helping of his crabby attitude, she fired back.

"Little Miss Christmas? How original. Aren't you supposed to be destroying snowmen or putting itching powder into the mall elves suits or something?" She went over to the front door and rotated the open sign to closed.

"I would but I have to be here since my boss, absolutely loves this bakery. He wouldn't consider going to the place on Third street even though it is way closer," Sam muttered.

"Eew. The bakery on Third sells week old muffins. No wonder you would prefer to go there," she took a long swig of French Vanilla then proceeded to put a candy cane into it.

"Are you calling me a muffin?"

She nearly did a spit take with her drink. "A muffin? That's the best you think I could've come up with?"

Melody impatiently waited for him to speak.

"The word I would use would probably be one that a kid shouldn't hear," she placed her mug in her hands and swung her feet back and forth.

"I'm surprised you have a big enough vocabulary."

"You know what?" Sam could practically see the steam billowing out of her ears. She grabbed the glass plate and slid the cookies into one of the bakery's to go bag. "Take your cookies, wherever they came from, because they did not come from here—"

"How could you possibly know that?" Sam's face remained a nonchalant gaze as he stared at the frustrated woman. Sam had to admit, it was pretty funny.

She crushed one of the them in her hands.

"See, that wasn't very nice," he titled his head, as he sarcastically smiled.

She put the crushed cookie remains onto the counter. "Look at it."

"As you can see I am," He snapped, slowly rising out of his chair to give the dust a peek.

"Do you see those tiny specks? Those pieces of green and pink?" she sifted through the mess with her fingers.

Once more, for the second time Sam's heart stopped—but just for a moment as he stared at the girl. He had to admit, she was more than what met the eye. No one and he meant no one, ever noticed the tiny specks in the cookie before. Those tiny specks as she had put it, weren't specks. They were little magical pellets that could turn the meanest Grinch into the nicest of lads.

Funny, they seemed to have the opposite effect on her. Or rather he had the opposite effect on her. Ever since he had said he hated Christmas, it seemed as if fate had supercharged them together.

"I see em," he snarled.

"Good," she triumphantly wiped her brow. "Because we here at Merry Bakery do not sell cookies with specks in them. "

"Fine, you got me! My mom bakes them."

She picked up a cookie and bit into it."These cookies taste like—"

"Shoot! That reminds me I gotta get going," Sam jumped up from his seat and proceeded to grasp the door handle.

"You can't leave! Do you not see the blizzard out there, you crazy buffoon?" She threw her hand in the direction of the door.

"Why do you care?"

"I-I don't," she averted looking at him. " I just don't want to get a lawsuit on my hands," she tried to convince Sam but really it was as if she were trying to convince herself.

"Because you love me so much, I'll stay."

"You wish. Besides I don't care if you go outside and freeze your tail off. Either way I get paid," she collapsed in the soft red recliner by the bookshelf.

"Harsh." It felt like Sam had been punched in the gut.

She selected a book from the shelf, with the picture of a Christmas tree on the cover. She skimmed through it, realizing she had read it before.

Sam sauntered over to where she sat, her head lifting up to meet his as he tried his hand at one of these books. He tossed a book on the floor, one after the other which caused Melody to freeze and gasp in utter horror.

"What are you doing?"

Sam ignored her, giving the books his own synopsis as they continued their way down. "Cliche, read it all before, not another one."

She marched up to him, seizing them off the floor. "These are classics, you sir are a destroyer of art!" Melody pointed a book in Sam's face, causing him to step back.

"Don't call me Sir. You remind me of my father. Call me Sam."

"Well Sam, if that's even your real name, please have some respect."

"I do have respect. I didn't call you a frustrated, loud, annoying, opinionated ball of fire that likes to control things."

Her hands wrapped around her torso as she found the ceiling. Tears pricked at her eyes.

"I'm sorry, I didn't mean it," Sam didn't know what to do or what to say. "I'm a jerk."

"Darn right you are! Anna told me not to stay away from you, but no," she chuckled a sad sob, "I just had to continue the conversation with you."

He briskly turned around, feeling the inside of the brick wall. "I didn't mean it. It's just that this time of year brings out the worst in me. I can't explain it."

"Try," she countered back, a heavy sigh erupted from her lips.

A blanket of darkness fell on the room, cutting any chance of an explanation. "It's a good thing you brought this," Sam removed the flashlight from my back pocket.

No response came from her direction.

He moved closer to her, knowing that she could feel his presence. "I--uh guess there's no point in leaving now."

"You think?" A snarky comment arose from the another part of the room.

"How are you doing that?" Sam wondered, noticing her shift in the room.

"Doing what?"

"Moving around in the dark."

"LIsten Sam, I know this place like it's the back of my hand."

"In that case, could you show me where the washroom is."

"Through that door," she pointed.

After a second, she realized her mistake and took his hand. "Here, I'll show you."

BABY, IT'S TOO COLD OUTSIDE

"Here, you look like you're freezing," Melody reached over to the ottoman, lifting the cover to reveal storage and a plush blanket.The quilt fabric brushed through her fingers as she extended her arm towards him.

"Thanks," Sam wrapped the cozy blanket over his body and stared at her as she returned to her book. He couldn't believe he had actually knocked her over, looking back on it. She seemed like someone he would have noticed.

"If you're done staring," she quipped as Sam's face turned as red as a tomato, "grab a book."

"I'd rather not," A wave of nostalgia washed over him as he tilted his head towards the shelf.

"How about I tell you a story instead?" Her eyebrows lifted as she considered his gesture.

"Why?" she leaned over so now her head was upside down with her feet resting on the inside of the chair.

"Because you look bored reading those books. I can tell you've spent all waking hours of the night reading them."

"You get all of that from a blank expression?" she adjusted her body, getting a good look at him as the candle burned weakly.

"A blank expression is one of the most detailed canvases." He saw her eyes flick over in interest.

"Continue on," she put down her book and gave Sam the cutest smile he'd ever seen.

"Once there was a young boy who dreamed of exploring the world. Everytime he would talk about it, his eyes would shine like the Milky Way. One day in particular he wanders far from home--

Melody held her breath hanging on to every word that left his lips.

Continuing on, a strange burning sensation fills his eyes. It's not until Melody is sitting beside him, that he notices he is crying.

"Sam, are you okay?" she follows the direction his head makes when he turn away from her.

"Why would you ask that? Of course I'm fine."He soon realizes he's having a conversation with a wall, when he notice her presence is gone.

"Melody?" Sam croaks out, startled at how his voice rings out into the quiet bake shop with just two of them inside.

"I'm right here Sam," she reassures him as a cup of French Vanilla is placed in his hand. Piping hot, the taste brings comfort to his cold body.

"It's alright you don't have to finish the ending. How about I tell you the time I biked to Sunset Village?"

"I'd like that very much Melody."Sam's hand grazes over hers and immediately there are butterflies in his stomach.

"Alright so it all started when my friend Clara--"

Sam droned out-- not purposefully I might add-- hearing the name Clara. The sugarplum, lavender dress twirled around in the town's square. He remembered that memory from every Christmas day since the summer day he'd been born. His father always took him down to see the Nutcracker. He didn't care much for the sword fights, no-- it was all about seeing Clara finally get her happily ever after.He and Clara were good friends which was why he couldn't tell her that he was leaving.

Melody burst out in a deep fit of chuckles just as Sam pulled himself from his memories. "Somehow I ended up with flowers in my hair after rolling down a hill."

"Seems you had quite the adventure," Sam rested his chin on his hand and watched as her eyes lit up capturing him in her adventures.

"You should visit there sometime. I would like to take you up there whenever you know-- it's not snowing,"

"That'd be awesome. I'd love to see the flowers that would get stuck in your hair."

Both could feel themselves drawing closer to one another...

The back up generator roared to life causing her to move away-- almost as if she was restraining herself. She tucked a strand of hair behind her ears and shyly returned to her previous sitting arrangement.

"I uh...better go," Sam pulled the blanket off of himself and headed out into the wintry mess.

Sam could feel her gaze as he reached for the door handle. He expected her to call him back, to tell him to stay, but she didn't.

She remained frozen in her seat.

He braced himself for the cold, as his hands touched the metal doorknob. "I'm not dreaming of a white Christmas," he sighs.

A plastic card slipped out of his pocket just as the bell chimed. Melody saw as the card fluttered to the ground.

Watching him turn down the street, the words finally escaped from her lips. "Don't go."

She felt the smooth texture of the card as she brought it closer to her face, to examining it. Her eyes opened wide as she read the words that were written on it."Santa, baby."

(Santa Baby) Hurry Down the Chimney Tonight

She twiddled her thumbs, staring at the piece of paper with only red font. She read the words over again as she tried to understand it.

"Santa, baby? What could that mean?"

"Hey Melody," Merry called out to her from behind the counter. Melody's eyes hovered over the book that was currently in her hand. She couldn't concentrate on it though, because her thoughts were preoccupied at the moment. Bored, she sprang up ready for anything.

Merry smiled warmly, which instantly put Melody in a better mood.

"What is it Merry?" she grinned.

A pink box was placed in her hand. "I need you to take this box next door to the Veterinarian."

"Are you trying to bribe Mr. Mulconey?" Melody wiggled her eyebrows. For the past few months, they'd been trading shy glances and a little too much giggling, if you asked her.

"No," she nonchalantly nudged Melody. "I remembered that these are his favourite, plus the weather's been badly lately and he could use some cheering up."

"Uh huh," Melody replied hiding her laughter.

Often on her shift she would pause to see them giggling and laughing and talking about the day. Often times she would watch as a hand grazed another, and sighed at how sweet they were to one another. This reminded her of...

Here she was trying to make sense of it all. Could it really be true? No, no that would be absurd! Right? She bit her lip as the cold weather nipped at her toes. Could the man that she knew for less than a week really be Santa Claus? I mean he was pretty young-- dashing even, he looked like he was her age. But then again," she pondered over the matter, "he could not even age."

As time ticked away, and after a few boxes of powdered jelly donuts, she decided once and for all to see him again-- to return the card of course and nothing more.

By the time she clocked out for her shift, she was certain of it.

But...

As the wind coloured her ears red while she turned the key closing up shop-- she decided it could wait.

Do You See What I See?

"Just couldn't stay away?" Melody mused staring at the Chocolate Labrador walking alongside Sam as the bakery door brought in morning sunlight. "You know, for someone who hates Christmas, you sure are here a lot."

Sam's jaw tightened as his ears picked up the word he detested.

"Buster," he looks down at the leash, "wanted to try the cupcakes."

"Uh huh," Melody crinkled her eyebrows. "Isn't it too early for sweets?"

"You could have cupcakes for breakfast," he countered, causing her to blush.

She ignored the tugging in the back of her mind, knowing that she had something to ask him.

"So you're a vet?" She mentally sighed as that wasn't the question she wanted to ask him. Why'd she say the silliest things?

"That would be correct," he bent down to give Buster a high five. Buster let out a bark, causing Melody to throw the straws that she was organizing in the air.

"Wait, so your boss is Mr. Mulconey? The Mulconey that Merry won't stop sending her cookies and donuts to?" She grabbed the numerous straws on the hardwood floor.

"That is correct," he repeated, scooping some up with his hands and returning them to her. "Mr. Mulconey likes the powdered jelly donuts very much. I've been here four times today just going back and forth."

Melody didn't say anything for a while. She was sad that she had missed Sam coming and going. Maybe they could've made small talk or even big talk-- just to pass the time.

He noticed her lull and decided to scratch Buster's fur.

Eyeing the adorable sight, she pulled her gaze away and began organizing the bookshelf.

Sam's head jerked up as he noticed something was bothering Melody. He wished he could just ask her what was wrong but he couldn't bring himself to.

The door to Sam's apartment swung open greeting him with heat that he so craved. Propping on to his bed, he kicked off his shoes and devoured the sandwich that he'd left in the fridge.

The TV screen blinked and instantly his ears were covered-- the jingling of bells and the Santa Claus of this world too much to handle.

He sighed as he moved to the kitchen, stuffing his face with comfort food. By the time he was finished, he had a spread of macaroni and cheese, chocolate cake, strawberry cheescake, BBQ chicken, burgers, milkshakes (vanilla of course), pizza, samosas and to top it all off: an ice cream sundae. It was more food than one person could eat. He didn't cook it of course-- the magic did. All he had to do was sprinkle a little dust and anything could appear. Too bad the one thing he wanted to appear, didn't.

It was also too bad he couldn't see through walls-- because a little somebody just had.

Doesn't He Know It's Christmas?

As Melody closed up for the night, she began her way home. Burrowing her head down, and tying the scarf around her neck she noticed something strange on the ground.

Now normally when she saw something yellow in the snow, she wouldn't dare touch it. But in this case, whatever was in the snow shimmered and shined, causing her to brush her mittens over it. It looked like glitter, so she thought that's what it was-- at first. She began walking again, the trail of golden dust laid out before her on the cold, white, fluffy, surface.

A realization hit her-- there were no craft shops for miles! How was there glitter on the ground? Another thought crossed her mind. She had seen this dust before! Yes, she was sure of it! When she was cleaning up after Sam had abruptly left, under the bar stool was the same dust. Maybe the two were related? But how? she wondered.

The trail led into an apartment building just a couple blocks away. Should she go in?

She slipped into the elevator unnoticed. Now what? She didn't know which floor the glitter was on.

By pure luck somebody got on, on the second floor. Peering past him, she saw the golden specks. "Excuse me sir," she pushed past him, just as the elevator doors were closing.

She wiped her brow. Phew! That was close! All through the hallway was decorated in Christmas cheer. There was tinsel, ornaments, even a Christmas tree in the middle of the hallway. All were brimming with Christmas joy-- except one door.

She followed the golden dust to the undecorated apartment door. Maybe it was Sam's? If it was, she wondered Doesn't he know it's Christmas?

Raising her knuckles, she paused. What if this was a mistake?

The door latch clicked and she scurried towards the elevator, ducking behind a wall.

Sweat rolled down her face as she heard the footsteps getting closer.

She held her breath and squeezed her eyes shut. Opening them a short while later-- she gasped.

Santa is Coming to Town?

Melody watched as the familiar silhouette entered the elevator.

As the doors slid closed, she saw it! The golden dust! Now why did Sam have it? None of it made sense-- not the card, not the shiny dust. He couldn't be-- no there was no way! Him, Santa Claus? He was the grouchiest person in the world when it came to Christmas. Surely he couldn't be the one to deliver toys.

Pushing the buttons, she hopped into the next elevator, trying to find where he had gone. She ran out in the freshly fallen snow, almost losing sight of Sam's footprints.

Panting, she spotted his trademark scarf blowing in the night air. She was careful to keep her distance, she didn't want to startle him.

He turned into a snowy clearing, bramble bushes and bare trees garnished the forest against the purple nightfall.

Melody held her breath as she entered further into the forest. She couldn't see where she was going. Only the crunching of Sam's feet guided her. Wanting to turn back, she realized she couldn't. Not only because she had a job to do (delivering the card), but also because she was lost.

Everywhere she turned, looked exactly the same.

Suddenly, a spark shot into the sky, both scaring her and exciting her. She decided the only logical thing to do was follow it.

Sprinting towards where she had saw the light, what she faced left her with more questions than answers.

She could just make out the large object in the distance.

The object had red trim, swirling designs and stood tall. Huge was definitely an underestimation when staring at the monster of an object.

Her mittens glided across the metal and wood furnishings. In her haste, she had totally forgotten about Sam. She had all the more reason to, as her curiosity descended over her.

Marveling over the sleigh, she hadn't the smallest thought of how it had ended up here-- in the middle of the woods. Had it broken down? Had the owner misplaced it somehow?

Melody chortled as she realized how silly the last thought was! This sleigh was a honker-- surely no one would misplace it.

She was so enchanted in it-- the same way Sam had been when he first laid eyes on her. But she didn't know that.

Climbing into it, or should I say falling into it? She was left in a rather uncomfortable position. The only thing cushioning her fall was the soft material from the seats.

Groaning, she quickly sat up to find annoyed yet surprised eyes frowning into her own. She gave a cheeky smile, hoping he wouldn't be mad.

"What are you doing here?" Sam scowled, startled by her sudden drop- in.

"Oh you know," she brushed herself off as he helped her up and out of the sleigh, "just out for a stroll."

"In the forest?" his eyebrows raised as he stared at the flustered girl trying so hard to make up an excuse.

"Hey, you were doing the same thing!" she pointed out.

"So you admit that you were following me?" He folds his arm waiting for her best excuse.

"I was not! Like I said I was taking a stroll through the forest!" she stretched her arms out wide, showing him the forest around them.

"If I did believe that-- which I don't, why would you be exercising in the night?" he furrowed his brow trying to figure out which was more confusing: this girl or his love life?

She shrugged, not delving too much in to it. "It helps me think." She was getting pretty good at this lying thing, she thought to herself.

She kicked the bottom of the sleigh with her foot. "You know for someone who is Santa Claus, you sure aren't jolly."

Sam's heart stopped. "Pfft. I'm not Santa Claus. That's preposterous! Why would you think that?" a nervous chuckle left his lips.

"Um...I don't know...the sleigh?"

"There is no sleigh."

"Right behind you. I should know I'm the one who fell into it."

Sam cracked up with laughter. "Oh yeah, you did."

"Laugh it up," she commanded. "Very mature."

And so he continued on.

"Are you finished?" she checked her imaginary watch.

He pretended to zip his lip and after a short chuckle, he nodded.

"Back to the sleigh," she said but was cut off.

Quick as a whip, Sam blew some of the glitter that Melody had seen earlier. Instantly the sleigh disappeared.

"How did you--! What the--! That is so cool!" she clapped her hands in delight and amusement.

"Oh you think that's cool?" Now he was show boating but Melody was much too busy not focusing on that."Watch this."

Using two fingers, he whistled a merry tune-- a contrast to the grumpy one he sang earlier. Instantly three reindeers appeared.

She smiled a smug grin. "You were saying you weren't Santa Claus?"

Now he turned red. "You tricked me!"

"What? Me, trick you? That has got to be the craziest thing I've ever heard. Well more crazy than seeing Santa Claus. I never even knew Santa Claus was actually real--"

He cleared his throat. "I'm not Santa Claus."

"But you--the sleigh--the reindeer!" she stammered as the moon rose into the sky.

"I'm not Santa Claus," he paused.

"But--"

"Okay," he returned to repairing the sleigh and slid under it, screwing with some bolts.

"Were you the one who lit that fuse?" she crouched down on the snow, where only his torso peeked out from underneath the sleigh.

He rolled out from under it, giving Melody his undivided attention. "Yeah. Why do you ask?"

"Thanks."

Understanding what she referred to and knowing that he was right about her following him, he gave her a warm smile.

"I found this," she began fishing through her pocket until she found what she needed. "I think this belongs to you," she placed the card in his hand.

"My card! I've been looking all over for it!" he beamed with joy and squeezed her into a giant hug. "Where'd you find it?"

"You dropped it," she replied feeling warm and fuzzy after he released her.

"Thanks, you don't know what this means to me," he replied.

"What does Santa Baby mean?" she wondered, cupping her hand with her mouth, finally sputtering the question.

"What?" Sam turned red.

"Santa Baby," she repeated.

"Oh that. That's a typo," he showed her the card, so she could read it over. "It's supposed to say Santa's Baby," he scratched his head.

"Santa's Baby? So that means--"

"I'm his son," Sam replied.

Walking In a Winter Wonderland

"You?" she exclaimed, breathless. Her mouth hung open, as she sighed in disbelief. "But you're the grumpiest person ever! How could you be the jolly man's son?"

She took a step towards him, resting her hand on his cheek. "But you're so human-like. You could pass for 18!"

"First of all, I never used to be the grumpiest person ever," he replied dryly. "It sort of happened over some time. Second, thanks?"

A smile crept across his face. "You could blame my aging on my boyish charm and good looks."

Melody rolled her eyes, but there was a wide grin on her face. "Right."

"I'm serious. Well that and being a magical creature-- or a descendent of one, comes with it's perks. For example, the ability to look any age you want."

"So you can look like anything?"

"Not exactly," Sam stared up at the stars. "You have to go through a Council, which includes the Easter Bunny, the Tooth Fairy, my father--"

"You know the Easter Bunny?" Her pupils dilated and her grip on Sam's arm intensified.

"Uh... yeah," he scratched the back of his neck. When did she gain the powers of Thor? The only reason why he knew of the Avengers, is because he had seen them on the tv last night.

"Can you get me free chocolate?"

"Asking the real questions, are we Melody?" he mused, seeing her ebullient demeanor.

"Yes. So can you?" she beamed, hoping he would say yes.

"I might be able to pull a few strings," Sam teased as she jumped in delight.

"If I knew you liked chocolate so much, maybe I would have brought some when I came down to Earth," he grinned.

"Why did you come to Earth? I remember you saying something about tv's and my world..." Melody trailed off.

"Wait? You heard that? I thought you hadn't!"

"No I was listening. I just didn't know what you meant. Now I do."

Melody put a hand in the air and waved it around.

"Yes, Melody?" Sam called on her.

"Let me get this straight, there is more than one world?" Surprise was evident in her voice.

"Yup, I don't live in this one, your Earth. We, being the family of all things Christmas, don't live in the North Pole like everyone thinks we do. The house in the North Pole is our vacation home for Earth 2."

"So you're telling me that there are alternate worlds? Like-- like in The Flash?" she petted one of the reindeer's snouts.

"Yes," he said slowly allowing her to digest all of this information. "Just one more. To make things easier, they celebrate Christmas on a different day."

"Oh that's Dasher," he replied, staring at Melody's interaction with the animal. "He likes carrots and apparently...you?" Sam now stood so that Dasher was in between the two of them.

"Aww. He likes me? Well Dasher has good taste," Melody replied.

Him and me both, Melody.

"So," Melody asks, "What brought you to Earth? Was it me?"

"You wish," he smirked, earning a snowball to his chest.

"Hey! That's cold!" he slid the snow off of his jacket.

"What are you gonna do about it?" she mocked his surprised expression.

"Well I could pelt you with snowballs," he countered packing some snow in his hands, "or I could have some fun."

"Fun? What fun?" The way he snickered left her uneasy.

"Wouldn't you like to know?"

"That would be the general consensus," she stated sarcastically, as she leaned against the sleigh.

"Maybe--"

"Yes?"

"Maybe I could tell you if you're on the nice list. I should know, being the jolly man's son and all. Or and you'll get a kick out of this one--" There was a mean glint in his eye." I could tell you if you're on the naughty list."

Melody gasped, worriedly. "I am not! Am I?"

"No, of course not," his hand touched her shoulder. "You? On the naughty list? I'll believe it when Dasher starts eating blueberries."

At the mention of his name, Dasher shook his head, causing the bells on his collar to jingle.

"Dasher doesn't like blueberries?"

"Not in the slightest. He's allergic. The last time my dad gave Dasher blueberries, we had to move to another house. It was toxic."

"Remind me to give Dasher blueberries the next time you anger me," Melody joked causing Sam to frown.

"Are you sure you're on the nice list?"

Melody guffawed. "Yes, I wouldn't have given you free cupcake samples if I wasn't."

"So you were bribing me, were you?"

"Bribing, sharing-- it's really all the same," she shrugged.

"Melody, you surprise me," he stepped closer, closing their proximity.

"That's a good thing?"

"Always," Sam pressed his forehead to hers.

"It's so nice under the stars," Melody said in awe as they sat in the sleigh.

"Yeah. I come here to think," Sam looked over at her.

"About what?" Melody's breath trailed off into the cool night.

"My life and my choices."

Sam's chest rose and fell as he got that off his chest.

"You have the perfect life," Melody stared deep into his eyes.

Sam got up, and exited the sleigh, not saying a word.

"You have reindeer that come at the drop of a hat, you get free cookies. What more could you want?"

"You just wouldn't understand," Sam shook his head. He was beyond finished with this conversation.

"Then let me understand," she held onto his arm, after following him. Melody remained fixated on this magical being-- whatever you wanted to call him. She was determined not to let him escape so easily.

"The cookies aren't that great, especially when the parents don't make them. You can still taste bits of flour as you bite into them."

"Is that all?" Melody glanced at her nails, listening to Sam's sob story.

"You know what? If you're going to be insensitive, then-- then just forget it!" He stormed away.

"Sam wait! I'm sorry. It's just hard for me to separate what I've known for years to this-- whatever this is!" she threw her arms up in defeat. "Think about it, some guy I've met just a few days ago happens to be Santa Claus's son? That's ridiculous, right?"

"Glad I'm just some guy to you."

"Sam, you know that's not what I meant," she assured him.

"It sure sounded like it was," Sam tightened his jaw, narrowing his eyes.

"Just explain it to me. How could your life be so bad? What is it that makes your life so impossible?" she yelled. "All of our lives have some form of impossible. What makes yours so different?"

"My dad!" Sam fumed.

"Ooh, your dad is Santa Claus, so what?" Melody pressed him further.

"My dad, the one you think is so great, is disappointed in me! Okay?" Sam's voice broke as he kicked some snow. "The man who epitomizes happiness and cheer and...and giving, is disappointed in his own son!"

"Sam that can't be true," Melody felt tears brimming, but she was adamant on not letting them fall.

"Only you would say that. My dad, he doesn't respect my career choices." Sam wiped his tears away with the back of his sleeve.

"But you love being a veterinarian," Melody said, startled by Sam's confession. She had never before seen him so angry, so hurt and so vulnerable. It broke Melody's heart to see her boyf-- an important person in her life so alone. "Come, sit with me," she eased herself into the snow.

Sam couldn't say no to her puppy eyes, no matter how hard he tried. He plopped down beside her, nervous for her to speak.

Melody placed his hands into her own. They felt like icicles!"Why are your hands so cold?"

Sam shrugged, putting up a silent barrier in between them.

"Fine, if you won't talk, I will," she huffed.

She cleared her throat as loudly and as long as she could, causing Sam to cover his ears.

Melody began humming a tune, which caused Sam to slowly bring his hands down. "Which song is that?"

"It's called Winter Wonderland."

"I like it," his face remained still, towards the direction of the forest.

"Sam, please tell me why being the son of a magical creature is so bad," she sighed as her head found his shoulder.

Sam didn't move a muscle. It was the first time he and Melody had gotten this close. She could make him feel as though he was on top of the world, or angry like a raging bull. And to be honest-- he didn't even mind. He internally sighed as he realized he was falling for her.

"My dad, he's very particular. He likes things done his way. Hence the reason why he's the only one to deliver presents by himself on Christmas," Sam wrapped his arms around her.

Melody scooted closer to him, enjoying his warmth. "Oh, I see. Can I ask you something?"

"Sure Mel."

"Mel?" she gazed up at him. "Is that what you're calling me now?"

"I..uh..."

"I like it," she affectionately laughed.

"Back to the question. So all the time in the movies where Santa has a daughter, that's really you?" she giggled.

"Very funny. But no, I actually do have an older sister. She's somewhere living out her dream of being an architect."

"Let me get this straight," Melody yawned. "She gets to live out her dream and you don't? That's not fair," her arms crossed her chest.

"Life's not fair Mel," Sam huffed, reminding himself of the argument he and his dad had prior to him coming here.

"Do you--do you still talk with your dad? Melody wondered.

"Not since last Christmas," Sam felt a pang of homesickness that he tried so hard to bury deep inside.

"Why not?"

Sam gritted his teeth. He was starting to grow annoyed at all of these questions. "Because Melody, we had a huge fight about everything. He wanted me to take over the family business--"

"But why couldn't your sister do it? She's older," Melody suggested.

"Mel, my dad is old fashioned. He'd prefer a man to do the job," Sam turned away.

"Well that's just--he can't-- I'd like to give him a piece of my mind," she stood up.

"Easy there, firecracker. Settle down," he flashed a coy smile and patted the snow where she had previously sat.

"I hate it when you do that," she turned crimson as a strawberry in summer.

"I, on the contrary love it," he nudged her as she returned to her seat.

"But that's not fair!"

"You've said that for the second time now," Sam huffed.

"But it's not, believe me!"

"No, I believe you, Mel. It's not. I--I don't want to be the next Santa. I really don't. I like being a veterinarian. It brings me so much joy just to see their tails wagging. Melody it's the best feeling in this world, in any world."

"Is that why you hate Christmas so much?" Melody asked watching as Sam wiped his nose.

"Exactly. What if I don't want to be the next Santa Claus? My dad just doesn't understand. That's why I hate Christmas, it's a reminder of what I can't have. Ever since I was old enough, he's been butchering me to become the next Santa Claus. And he brought down the sleigh this year to see if I'd take the bait. I'm not gonna do it Melody. I finally had enough and I...I left."

"Listen Sam, you can be anything that you want to be. Look at me," she instructed.

"That's easy for you to say. You're just a human, you can do whatever you want."

Melody's voice cracked, her tears dripping onto the white snow. "I'm just a human?"

Christmas Isn't Christmas without the One you Hate

Her stammering filled the silence as Sam reached out to her.

Opening his mouth to speak, only hot breaths of air greeted the midnight sky.

Her arms ran the length of her winter coat, grateful for the feeling of security that seemed to be fleeting at this very moment.

She had felt close to Sam-- closer than she'd ever been with anyone, but now his words distanced them like the chasms of the Grand Canyon.

The temperature dipped and so did her fondness of the magical boy with every second.

Pleading with his heart and eyes, he took one more breath. Breathing was all both could do. Both could feel the rifts and ripples of each other's words.

Once again she felt the restraints of her heart, rising to the surface. She didn't take another step towards him. Even though the snow rapidly descending from the sky bruised her cheek, what he had said bruised her even more.

Why did it seem like every time he broke down her walls, something would build them back up again higher and stronger?

The moment they shared at the bakery over piping hot scones and a warm fireplace, entered his mind as he remembered how she had pulled away from him.

There was a fire kindling between him and Melody and Sam knew it, he just couldn't unwrap it.

He knew it because he had seen it. The same passion was inside of his friend Clara and her Nutcracker. It was in every dance, every smile and in every lingering gaze.

"Melody, that is not what I meant. You know that," he hung his head in shame. "Please tell me that you know that."

His words were lost as the howling wind circled them, drowning him out.

Sam's sadness melted into despair as Melody finally spoke."How could I possibly understand? I'm just a human anyway, right?" she shrugged and petted Comet's snout.

What Sam replied, rattled Melody's core. "You're right."

Melody bit the inside of her cheeks, hoping the ache would distract her for the storm that was quickly brewing. "I'm what?"

Her heart had hoped she had misheard him, that somehow he was referring to something else. The silence sprinkled a tiny fledgling of hope, but his words they told a different story. "You are just a human. You wouldn't understand what it would be like to be in my shoes.

The problems that you consider catastrophic in your tiny, human world don't even hold a candle to mine."

She brushed the salty tears and snow from her rosy cheeks. "How can you stand here and say that?"

Internally he knew what he was saying was wrong, there wasn't any doubt about it. However, the hurt that was protruding from his heart blinded him and froze any compassion he once had.

He gulped, the dryness of his throat scratching him adding to the harshness of his words. "Because Little Miss Christmas, it's true. You wouldn't last a day in my world. "

Pain shot through her as though she'd been stabbed by a long shard of ice. "Oh poor you! You think that everyone should grovel at your feet just because you so happen to be Santa's son. Well welcome to Earth where you suck it up and deal with your problems instead of running away to the nearest world that you can find!"

Sam huffed as his patience was thinning. "If you think my life is so easy, why don't you do it?"

The burlap sac filled with the magical dust stopped just inches short of her rubber boots as Sam chucked it at her.

"Fine! I will!" she angrily grabbed it off of the wet snow and put it under her arm. "Anything else, Mr. I-Hate-Christmas?"She smiled in satisfaction knowing she was getting a rise out of him.

He snatched the Santa's hat out of his satchel and threw it in her direction, luckily she caught it this time.

Her eyes remained on him as he stalked up to her. She couldn't move as her feet decided they had a mind of their own . She hadn't ever seen Sam's face turn that shade of red, ever.

His body diverted from his previous path and turned to the reindeer who had their faces on the ground. He shackled the reins and made sure they were secured to the sleigh. "Have at it. They're all yours. Oh and Mel?"

She narrowed her eyes as her head disobeyed her and followed his voice. "What Sam?" she gritted her teeth.

"Try not to break anything," he bared his pearly whites.

He stalked off leaving her with her hands full of responsibilities and for once, he was glad he didn't have any.

Will I Be Home for Christmas?

The night sky filled with dazzling wonder became her ceiling as she laid her head back.

The reindeer became rambunctious so she hazily got up and fed them some carrots and apples that were left in the sleigh. "What did I get myself into guys?"

Truth be told, she didn't know if the reindeers were male or female. Her knowledge was limited due to all the holiday stories that she heard as a kid.

Curling up with the blanket left on the seat, she wondered if the stars were really aligning. Was this fate, her ending up in this predicament?

"He wouldn't leave me, would he?" she spoke to the sky, wondering if she was lucky enough to see a shooting star. She really needed one.

Time passed by but Melody wasn't sure how much time passed. She had no concept of time seeing as she didn't have a watch or a clock. Where would she put a clock anyway?

These were just some of the thoughts that ran through her head.

She didn't know when or how but soon she was slumbering mess, with her hair matted and tangled.

The fact that she was sleeping in a sleigh slipped her mind as she was as tired as a sleepy dwarf.

She also wondered if Sam's world had dwarves as well. It would be possibly nice to meet a dwarf, maybe she'd meet Snow White too.

Deeply entranced in sleep, she was startled by a crackling sound. It didn't sound anything like the fire that she and Sam had sat by a few days ago. Static erupted from the sleigh's radio.

She rubbed her eyelids coming face to face with same pitch dark that she had left only a few short hours ago when she had first closed her eyes.

"Sam?"

She leaned forward, straining her ears to hear whatever the voice was saying. Only, it wasn't Sam's voice.

Melody sulked as she allowed herself to fall deeper for the magical boy. She fiddled with the knob trying to turn it off or at least turn the volume down.

She sighed as she stared down at the detached knob in her mittens. "Sam is gonna kill me."

She whistled as she nonchalantly kicked it under the seat. "Let's just leave that there."

The cheery voice made its debut once again, which caused Melody to crawl towards it. Slowly the look on her face changed from calmness to worry.

"Attention attention! Sleigh to the ready!"

"Well that can't be good," Melody thought to herself.

———

"Dasher, Dancer, Prancer, Vixen, Comet, Cupid, Donner, Blitzen and Rudolph head to the sleigh! Tonight we'll see what Sam is made of," the voice from the radio continued on.

Melody swallowed the lump in her throat.

"I'm so proud of him," Santa muttered, forgetting the radio was on. "He's finally taking initiative with the sleigh this year. I'm glad he's forgetting all about the Veterinarian dream. It's time he got his head on straight."

The girl's heart was pounding because as she would greatly like to point out, she was not Sam.

"How did I get into this mess?" she smacked her head with her hand.

Santa's voice startled her once more. "Attention attention! Christmas has begun!"

Oh Candy sticks!

The rest was a blur as wooziness overtook her.

When she came to, a scream escaped her lips as the ground beneath her grew farther and farther away.

Silent Night

Sam stomped all the way home, steam practically spouting from his ears. Slamming his satchel on the ground by his bedside, he let out a bellowing scream.

He put his head in his hands and slid them down his face. "That girl can enrage even the calmest bull," he sighed.

He picked up his alarm clock, as he tucked himself in to bed. His head fell back in frustration as he realized he would have to get up early in the morning to walk the dogs.

"Maybe Cooper can take one for the team."

Cooper was Sam's favourite coworker since he started working at Paws Veterinarian Clinic. Cooper teased Sam when he found out where he'd been that night of the blizzard.

"You're telling me that you don't have feelings for this girl next door?" Cooper said as he piled the boxes into the stock room.

"Not in the least bit," Sam passed the boxes to him. He fumbled causing one of the boxes to hit the floor.

"You've never dropped a box before," Cooper bent down and picked it up, never breaking eye contact with Sam as he did so. "Boy, this girl's more trouble than I thought," Cooper shook his head, playing on Sam's emotions.

"Hey, she's not trouble!" Sam barked, to which Cooper gave Sam a coy smile.

"Oh shut up and move those boxes," Sam pointed the dozen boxes lined up in the narrow hallway.

"Don't deny it Sam. You've been acting strange-- sort of lovestruck since you went over to that bakery. More strange than usual if you ask me--"

"Well I didn't--'

"I'll take that crass attitude to confirm my theory," Cooper winked. "But seriously it's like you're not even from this world. Do you remember when you first came bustling through that door a year ago?"

Sam heaved the boxes, not paying attention to Coop.

"You had the scariest, most fearful frown I had ever seen. But then you warmed up when I first brought Scott in and now again with Maggie."

Sam glared at Cooper. "It's Melody."

"Now is no time for writing a song, Sam."

Sam rolled his eyes. "Melody. Her name's Melody."

"Oh. You remember her name, eh?" Cooper gave Sam a light jab in his ribs.

"Okay Coop, you've made your point." Sam pushed him away.

"I have, haven't I?" Cooper asked.

"Yes," Sam groaned in annoyance. He hated being wrong-- it was the same characteristic he shared with his father.

"So what are you going to do about it?"

By now, all of the boxes were in their right place and they had each stopped to continue their conversation by the water fountain.

'What do you mean?"

"Come on, Sammy. You know what I'm talking about. Go see this Maddie."

"Melody," Sam corrected.

"Whatever. Go see her or else I will."

"You wouldn't," Sam countered, sizing Cooper up.

"I might, I heard she makes the best gingersnaps this side of town."

"You're skating on thin ice Coop," Sam crumpled the plastic water cup and tossed it into the nearby garbage can.

"And you're not accepting your true feelings," Coop poked Sam's chest.

"That's easy for you to say--"

"Because I have a girlfriend?" Coop shifted his weight to his other foot. "Snow and I have been together for two years. Don't you think it takes time and work to get to where we are now?"

"I guess." Sam called out before walking away.

Looking back on it, Sam had to admit he was pretty stubborn.

He also had to admit that right now, he was a little peckish. Well, more than a little peckish, more like ravenous.

He decided tonight was not the night to stay in and sulk.

"I knew this place was warm," Sam could just taste the deli sandwiches as his mouth watered.

The traditional restaurant walls were replaced with horizontal, rustic wooden logs and a western carpet stretched out onto the floor.

A long counter folded into a square with the bartender inside, was the perfect place for loud conversations as those tired from standing took a seat on the outskirts.

Sam gave the hostess a genuine smile as she placed a menu down where he folded his legs over a rustic, cherry wood, chair.

She sent a flirty wink his way which Sam didn't enjoy taking, but wanting to be polite returned a kind grin.

"See anything you like?" she asked returning a short while later to see how he was doing.

"This sandwich looks good," he replied, not looking at her.

"That's our special. Coming right up," she swiftly turned around walking towards the swinging kitchen doors.

"Much obliged," Sam tipped his head.

Sam stepped out into the brisk winter elements and zipped up his coat. The aftertaste from the tangy sauce of the sandwich didn't sit well with his palate. During the course of his meal, he downed several glasses of water as if his life depended on it. Still, the taste lingered. Sam decided the best way to restore his tastebuds was to eat something sweet.

Across the street, in between the pet clinic and the laundromat, stood the pink safe haven he'd come to enjoy.

He stepped out onto the street, but quickly took a step back. It wasn't just because a driver yelled obscene things at him, but because he wasn't sure if he could go in.

The clock in the town square rung loudly for all to hear. Sam squinted to get a better look at the large tower. He quickly peeled himself off of the bone-chilling bench he'd been sitting on for half an hour and trudged in the mile-high snow, to the only light source awake in the sleepy town.

The sunny woman dressed in an apron smiled as she adjusted her glasses. Her red curls and cherub face welcomed Sam gladly.

Sam wrapped his arms around her and gave her a tight squeeze. "Hi Merry. How ya doing?"

"Fine now that you walked in," she chuckled patting him on the back.

Peering over her shoulder, he saw the blonde ringlets he had grown accustomed to. He watched as the woman placed marshmallows in her mug of cocoa. Sugar danced from her fingers into the mug that she brought to her lips.

Sam politely broke away from the hug and leaned on the corner adjacent from the woman who seemed not to notice him.

He was afraid to say anything-- he didn't know how to start. He had left a path of destruction with his words, like rubble after an earthquake.

"Sam," Merry tapped his shoulder.

"Hmm," he pulled his eyes away from the white, glossy counter and looked at Merry.

"Please can you do me a favour?"

"Sure."

Merry had become like a friend to him in the recent days that he'd known her, She was genuine and real and had a fantastic sense of humour. It also helped that Sam had peeked on the nice list and saw her name there. He didn't mind helping her out, considering he wasn't busy at the moment.

"Will you-- and this is important-- take this box over to your boss? I-I know it's late, but I also know that some nights he stays late well into the wee hours of the morning-- and I know you don't work here but--"

"Say no more Merry. I'd be happy to," Sam waited as Merry put the box into his hand.

"Powdered jelly donuts are his favourite," Merry called out as Sam exited the sweet shoppe.

"He says he appreciates them, Merry," Sam kicked the snow from his boots onto the black carpet.

"That's good," she played with her hands, and went back to cleaning up.

"I know this is none of my business, and I-I don't mean to intrude but... is there something going on between you two?" Sam slipped off his hat and wrung it in his hands.

"No, that's preposterous," Merry cheeks turned the colour of the berry that accompanied mistletoe. "What--"

"No need to get flustered Merry, it's ok. I won't tell him. Plus, and I'm not playing matchmaker or anything. That's cupid's job," he whispered the cupid sentence. "But I've seen the way he lights up whenever I send something over or...or when he stops by for a snack break. And something tells me he's not just here for the snacks."

"Really?" Merry beamed.

"Oh yeah," Sam said.

"For your good efforts, you deserve something to eat."

"I-I couldn't," Sam insisted.

"It's on the house," Merry's eyes sparkled with kindness, as Sam glanced through the display case.

"You know what, I heard the powdered donuts have a pretty good review," he laughed.

"So did I," Merry placed a few in a sparkly green paper bag.

Nostalgia hit Sam like a ton of bricks as the bag reminded him of the green and red outfit Melody had first worn when she had just met him.

He popped the tiny round donut hole into his mouth. "Oh my gosh, these are delicious!" He without haste, put another one in his mouth.

"Melody usually makes them. But she hasn't shown up for closing. She usually takes care of that too. It's not like her," Merry placed one hand one her hips and even though she wasn't looking at him, Sam could feel eyes boring into the back of his head.

Sam gave Merry a quizzical look. "But isn't that Melody over there?"

He gestured with a pen that was on the counter and pointed it to the blonde haired girl.

"No that's Claire, she's one of our new hires."

As Claire turned around, Sam saw that Merry was right. "Merry, I got to go. I've made a huge mistake. Thanks for the donuts, they're awesome!"

Sam picked up his jacket and rushed out the door.

Is it the Most Wonderful Time of The Year?

Sam ran through the forest, where he had left her. He tripped and silently scolded himself as he fell.

The moon wasn't even as bright as it was moments ago, causing him to hit his shin on a lowered and bent tree branch.

He slid under branches, pushed twigs and ended up not a happy camper as some snow seeped into his boots.

"The things I do for this girl," he muttered to himself.

He had just set foot deeper into the woods when he heard the sound of a motor revving.

He stopped in his tracks, realizing the sound must have come from the sleigh.

"Yes I got it to work!" he cheered to himself.

He cupped his hands around his mouth trying to keep them warm, still descending further. "Where is she? She was here two hours ago."

He knew that was bad the moment he thought it. How could he leave her for two hours?

He could hear Cooper's smug voice, scolding him in his mind. "Sam you messed up."

"Oh no. No no no no, this can't be happening," he entered the clearing just as the sleigh took off. "Melody!" he called out.

But she was too far away to even hear him, let alone notice him.

Sam kicked the snow off of his already soggy boots. He counted on his fingers realizing the gravity of the situation before him."She has no training, no experience-- not to mention can she even shimmy back up a chimney? This is not good! What do I do?"

———

Stocking hung from the fireplace as Sam paced back and forth, underneath his father's stern gaze. The fire roared and so did his father's temper.

Sam gave the snow-white husky bounding towards him a good scratch behind the ears. "Hi, Aster. I've missed you." He picked up the little pup, and made a pouting face to his father. "You wouldn't yell with Aster around, now would you?"

Sam knew his father had a weak spot for animals. He also knew that his father had an explosive temper. The two didn't mix. Not only was Sam handsome (according to Melody) but he was also the expert in getting out of trouble.

"Aster, come here boy," Santa yipped. His son was not getting off scott free if he had anything to say about it.

"Aster," Sam said in a sing-songy voice. "It's a trap. Stay where you are. I'll give you a treat."

Aster licked Sam's hand as if agreeing with the idea.

"That's a good boy," Sam rubbed Aster's ears.

"Will you two stop fooling around?" Mrs. Claus walked in carrying a plate of freshly baked cookies. "Now Sam," she adjusted her glasses, "what did you do to that poor girl?"

"Me? I didn't do anything! She just took off with the sleigh that dad dropped in the middle of the forest..." Sam mumbled the entire sentence stuffing with face with cookies.

"She did WHAT?"

Sam could swear his mother had super hearing. He mumbled incoherently once more.

"Again...you did WHAT?" his mother smacked the plastic plate with the cookies onto the small coffee table adorned with a festive tablecloth. "So you're telling me that a human is driving the sleigh and not you?"

"That would be the general consensus," Sam replied sitting on the posh sofa cushion that was on the floor.

"Come on we have to help her!" Sam pleaded. His heart did that skippy thing it did when he saw properly made cookies. What was happening?

Santa told his wife to gather all of his things. Mrs. Claus put some cookies into a red sac and handed one to Sam and one to his father.

"Dad, aren't we forgetting something?"

Santa chuckled. "Right, my hat. How could I forget that? Thanks son."

"No. I'm talking about the bigger picture."

Santa tilted his head unsure of what his son was referring to.

"The sleigh..." Sam cleared his throat. "If Melody has the sleigh how are we going to get to her without one?"

"Number one Sam," Santa began, "now is not the time to be writing a song. Second, don't you think I have a spare?"

Santa walked over to a purple curtain just off the side of the living room. Pulling back the curtain, Sam gasped as his father nodded.

"Well...it looks...promising." Sam stared at the piece of dusty junk that once upon a time resembled a sleigh.

"It just needs a tune up. Will you help me?" Santa brushed off some of the dirt.

Sam leaned in and inspected the exterior of the sleigh. Springs were springing, bells not ringing and the golden rod for stepping into the sleigh was missing. "This is going to take a lot of work."

Santa dejectedly nodded. "It was a long shot. I guess there's no point now."

Then he did something that Sam never thought he would do--he apologized. "I'm sorry."

Those two words made Sam's heart swell.

"I'm sorry Sam. If I never pushed you to take over the family business, none of this would've happened. You wouldn't have held a grudge, and your girlfriend wouldn't be possibly halfway across the world by now--"

"Girlfriend? She's not my girlf--"

"Sam."

Sam turned to face his dad.

"Is she a girl?"

Sam nodded.

"Is she your friend?"

"Well, I guess."

"Then she's a girlfriend. Besides it's not like you've had one of those in awhile anyway," Santa chortled.

"Are we gonna work on the sleigh or not?" Sam awkwardly chuckled.

"You mean you'll help?"

"Have I ever said no?" Sam gave his dad an assuring grin. "Now let's paint the town Christmas."

Must Be Melody

"Let's paint the town Christmas," Melody adjusted the reins in her hand.

She had successfully delivered presents to one house-- luckily the child was an only child.

Sam was right about the chimney part. It was easier getting down, than shimmying up, which she would later come to realize.

Flurries flew in her face and her boots were soaked by the time she got to the second. "I don't know what Sam was complaining about. This job is not that hard!"

By the time she had gotten to the third, her feet were numb, her fingers were throbbing and she could barely speak because her mouth was frozen.

Other than some hitches in the road-- or should I say sky, Melody had gotten used to the gliding motion of the sleigh. Hoisting the heavy sac over her shoulder she exited the sleigh and hopped onto a roof.

Blue shingles and dirty gutters were all the rage with this house. Some twigs, branches, leaves and gritty water caused Melody to gag. "If I can just," she swallowed the heavy lump in her throat that threatened to come bubbling up, "get through this disgusting mess of a house, I can do anything."

"I hope she's alright," Sam drank a piping hot mug of hot chocolate. "But then again, if I know her like I do, she can do anything."

"It seems to me that you like this Melody," Mrs. Claus sat beside her son, who right now felt like he should be getting coal in his stocking.

"Is it that obvious?" Sam sighed as he placed the mug down and wrung his hands together.

"Yes," Mrs. Claus chuckled as she rubbed her son's back. "If I know you, you'll do the right thing."

"And what would the right thing be?" Sam sighed and looked into the eyes that resembled his.

"That's for you to decide," Mrs. Claus got up, just as her husband put the finishing touches on the old sleigh.

"I hate it when you say that. Can't you just tell me what's the right thing to do!" Sam groaned. "You're the parent, you're supposed to teach me right from wrong."

"If you're sitting here worried sick about Melody-- a girl you just met and you have a conscience-- then I've done my job," she smiled wickedly.

"And so have I," Santa beamed, "with this sleigh of course!" he rumbled with laughter.

"It's finished?" Sam lit up with cheer and holiday spirit, the most since the argument with his dad last year.

"Yes Sam. Now do we have everything we need?"

Sam nodded.

"Then, let's go save Christmas!"

"And Melody," Sam added.

As Melody climbed out of the chimney covered in soot, from her head to her boots, she flung the sac down and took a seat. Her hands were behind her to support her weight and her legs were bent at the knee. "Hey Rudolph, is it just me or is this bag getting heavier and heavier?"

Of course Rudolph only jingled his bells, which was more than what Melody had hoped for in response.

"Alright guys, let's head out. These presents aren't gonna deliver themselves," she stood up and carried the sac across the roof shingles. Her arm nearly snapped from all the tension. Rubbing the spot, she cried out in pain and decided it was best to drag the bag during the boisterous storm.

Her feet slid out from under her as she slipped on some ice covered with snow. Roof shingles met their early fate as they tumbled off the roof and scattered into pieces. She grasped onto the gutters (which she was thankful for at that moment, no matter how horrendous they were) and shut her eyes as she held on for dear life.

"Oh dear."

On the First Night of Christmas...

After getting the sleigh to fly, the father and son duo took to the skies.

"Oh where is she?" Sam said as they flew over a quiet neighbourhood. There were houses of every size and height in the small cul de sac.

"We'll find her Sam, just be patient," his father told him.

All Sam could taste was the snowflakes landing on his tongue. How he wanted to taste her lips on his lips-- even though they'd never kissed before. He wondered if they tasted like Christmas, which he had to confess he didn't entirely hate anymore.

Sam munched on a sugar cookie as he leaned his head out of the window. "Melody could be anywhere-- Rome, London even Jamaica!"

His father stopped the sleigh in mid air, causing the reindeers to screech to a sudden halt. A cool breeze fanned Sam's face causing him to sweep his hair out of his face. "What did you do that for?"

"Because if you don't calm down I will turn this sleigh around. Got it?" Santa's eyes softened as he saw his son's gloomy expression. He put the sleigh in neutral. "Look, I'm sorry. I just can't stand to see you this way all heartbroken over this girl. Where's your Christmas spirit?"

"She took it, along with my heart."

And with that, not a word was uttered until the next passing town.

"Can we stop for cheese fries?" Sam slid back into his seat. Sounds of hunger growled from his stomach. He was tired of sugar cookies, to the point that one look would send him puking over the next house.

"And miss Christmas? What an absurd boy! Just take some cookies from the bag that your mother gave you! Are you sure you're cut out for this job?" He sent Sam a suspicious glance as he reached into the bag himself.

"You already know the answer to that question," Sam answered.

Grumbling, he let the night air take his breath away as he stared at the moon. The marvelous sight had become his friend on this lonely night-- far away from his true friend-- the girl who managed to steal his heart.

"I know what that sigh means so I'll just ask my question. Is she a toy delivery expert?"

When Sam didn't respond, probably thinking that that was the most stupidest question his dad ever asked him, his dad spoke again.

"...Then I'm pretty sure she hasn't gotten that far."

———

Callouses on the insides of her hands caused her to wince in pain, as she tried to pull herself upwards. She looked down and instantly regretted it, closing her eyes as she saw how high up she was.

"Dancer, Dasher, Vixen, Rudolph help! Now! Please," she pleaded as adrenaline shot through her veins. She stammered and prepared herself for the worst. It was all she could do.

The shingles creaked and one broke in half as the reindeers trotted closer. Realizing what was happening, she commanded them not to come a step further. "I'll fall, stop right there."

They moved back happy that they weren't her.

Her fingers burned as she could only feel the throbbing sensation courtesy of the bone chilling cold. They felt as though they'd been slammed inside a door, not once, not twice but a dozen times.

Even her warmest clothing couldn't prevent Jack Frost from seeping into her bones, causing her to sneeze profusely. "If I get hypothermia it is all his fault."

And by him she wasn't talking about Frost anymore.

Her nose became as red as Rudolph's and now she really wished she was stuck inside a chimney. At least it would be warm.

Weeping loudly, she didn't care if the neighbours heard her, maybe they'd even help or even send a ladder. Searching the sky she reunited with the star she had seen when Sam had first abandoned her in the woods. "If anyone is listening, primarily you Santa, please hear me out. I know I'm too old for your presents and you might not hear this but if--" she sniffled, not wiping her nose because she needed all of her strength-- "if you do could you please grant me one special wish?"

"I think I see something," Santa exclaimed passing a house.

"What? I don't see anything," Sam got up out of his chair, which caused his father to pull him back down.

Could it really be her?

"Oh it's just a sneaky little racoon," Santa replied, wondering if he should have even said anything.

"Stupid racoon," Sam muttered.

"Over there!" Santa pointed, startling Sam out of his slumber.

"I'm up, I'm up!" Sam wiped the drool as it spilled from his mouth. "Did we find her?"

"Maybe."

Now Sam was alert and ready. He was determined once he found her to never let her go.

"Look on that roof over there. I see something but I can't quite make it out," Santa placed a hand above his eye trying to see if he could get a better look.

"Is that-- is that a person dangling from a house?"

"I think so," his dad answered. "We have to save them."

"But it'll reveal our secret," Sam protested. Everything they'd worked for would be gone in an instant if any mere mortal was to see them in real life.

"The people of this world already know we exist. Haven't you seen those impersonations of me at the malls around this time every year?"

"To be honest, I was trying to block that out."

"And why would you do that?"

"Because of the fight we had, the fight that caused us not to speak for a year. You know, the one about the rule that once I turn eighteen that I must take over the duty of Santa Claus? That rule?"

"I remember. Regardless of how you're feeling, that shouldn't get into the way of helping someone in need. Your mother and I taught you better than that."

"I know. I just..."

He stared his son down, locking his gaze. "It's the right thing to do."

"If you're still feeling uneasy, we'll just erase their memories," Santa pulled out the brown, burlap sac that was filled the glorious golden dust. "They won't feel a thing."

———

A heavy strain was felt from her wrists downward to her shoulders as they were the only thing keeping her from ending up like the shingles.

Discomfort rang throughout her body, and so did tiredness.

"Oh why did I have to meet that hater of Christmas," her mouth quivered and shivered and the frost of the night decorated her lips in swirls of icicles. "He has done nothing but ruin my life and now I'm going to die because of him!"

Seeing no end in sight, she said her final goodbyes. She said goodbye to her memories, when tears welled in her eyes. She choked out what was to be one of her last breaths, though she had a lot more to say. "Goodbye Sam."

A cough attacked her lungs and she ranted on. "What else has he given me besides frostbite, and something pleasant to look at. Whoa--"

Gravity took her into its arms.

She descended rapidly downwards, and felt her life-- her boring life-- flash before her eyes. The fact of the matter was, was that meeting Sam was one of the most exciting things that ever happened in her life. He was a challenge-- what with hating Christmas and all, but deep down he made the challenge fun.

As she fell, staring up at the reindeer as they made a whinnying sound, she passed by a window on the middle floor. She caught a glimpse of a girl writing a letter to Santa. Melody smiled remembering how little she was when she used to do that. It was like looking through a mirror except this girl had darker hair. She smiled as her mother came to the living room, helping the little girl put the card on the mantle and rested a plate of cookies on it.

Melody sighed dispirited as the memory of when Sam mentioned how fresh cookies weren't good when the parents didn't make them, flooded into her mind.

"I didn't even say goodbye."

On the last window, nearing her death she saw red.

My Grown-up Christmas Wish

Red-- the colour of stockings. The colour of a juicy apple in the summertime. A bold statement.

A colour that Melody was happy to see as her cheeks flushed pink. A blur, shiny as a Christmas ornament whizzed by. Whirling around, she tried to locate her surroundings but she was much too dizzy to figure it out. Shock rattled her bones as she realized she was alive.

Sam's murmuring in her ear made her eyelids flutter. She breathed a sigh of content as she rested her body onto his lap.

"Seems to me you've had quite the night," Sam said, sending a flirty grin her way.

She quickly brushed herself off, moving away from him, though she had to admit, she felt cold without his touch. "No thanks to you. I almost died!"

"I'm so sorry Melody. I shouldn't have gotten angry at you, it was stupid of me."

"You got that right!" she yelled crossing her arms.

"So this is the infamous Melody I've been hearing so much about," Santa tipped his hat towards her. "You gave this one," he shook his son by the shoulder causing Sam to glower at him, "quite a scare."

"I did?" Melody asked with a sly grin. She was definitely not going to let Sam live this one down. "You cared about me Sam?"

Sam shrugged. "Where else would I get powdered jelly donuts?"

"Well regardless," she gave him a forceful punch in the side of his arm.

"Ouch," Sam tended to the purple bruise that was now forming. "What was that for?"

"For leaving me dangling, not telling me how cold it could get delivering presents and once again for causing me to spend the night dangling from the side of a house!"

"I mean at least I gave you a fun night."

Melody's eyes widened at Sam's definition of the word fun. Baking, playing in the snow, shopping at the hardware store-- now that was fun. It was also not life threatening as Melody would like to point out.

"What would you have been doing?" Sam eyed her precisely, studying every bit of her. "Possibly closing up shop now and going home. Am I right?" He stared at the passing sky as he said this.

"That's not--"

"What...True?" Sam turned and she could have sworn she saw the ocean in his eyes.

"No," she pouted, frowning because maybe he knew her better than she had thought.

"That's not all I gave you."

"What are you talking about?" she asked trying to figure out his clever brain worked.

"I mean, I did give you something pleasant to look at," he grinned as he bit down on a sugar cookie.

"You heard that?" At this point in time she was thankful that her ears were red because she could blame it on the cold, instead of the fact that she was embarrassed.

"Loud and clear, Mel." He saw as her movements became flustered and she tried to hide her face. In a sing- songy voice he said, "You like me, you really like me."

"Oh shut up, magical boy."

"Magical boy?" Sam furrowed his eyebrows. "I like it."

Heat creeped up behind her ears, as she realized she had just revealed her secret nickname for him.

"Dang it! And here I was trying so hard not to like you," she quipped while looking down and seeing the Eiffel Tower. We're in France? How fast does this sleigh travel? Just a minute ago we were back in...

"You didn't try," he grinned down at her, enamoured by her curiousness for the world. To him, this was just any other tower, but to her it was like she had never seen something so beautiful.

"Neither did you," she scooted closer to him.

Again there was that pitter- patter in his chest that he felt time and time again when she was near him. Was he-- no it couldn't be possible-- there was no way he was in love! But then again... "Yeah I didn't," he shrugged and gave her a coy smile.

Santa cleared his throat. The two lovebirds were like deer caught in headlights as they forgot that he was even there. Melody sheepishly turned away from Sam as he stared at her wishing she would come back.

"Why are you always scooting away from me?"

"Because," she answered not wanting to get swept away by the blue currents she saw in his eyes. "This..." she gestured to everything around them, "could get taken from me in an instant."

"I don't understand," Sam shook his head. That doesn't make any sense.

"Look at it from my point of view. This is like a fairytale or like something you read in those books you threw onto the ground the night of the blizzard. It doesn't seem real. "

"Sam did what, Melody?" Santa raised one eyebrow and peered at his son who was now tugging on the collar of his jacket.

"Where's a rest stop when you need one, right Melody?" Sam softly nudged her, hoping his father's unsmiling gaze towards him would soon fade. Many nights he would find his dad in his study reading his nights away-- now he was a real bookworm. Sam had a feeling his father and Mel would get along well since she loved books.

"Continuing on," she stated. "It's like a dream-- all of it, magical creatures, flying in Santa's sleigh, and I'm afraid, I'm afraid that soon I'll wake up and it'll be gone."

"Don't worry Mel. I would never let that happen," he hugged her closer.

"Well, this all fine and dandy but if we don't hurry half of the world's children will not be pleased when they wake up next morning," Santa huffed.

"Don't the parents--"

Sam glared at Melody, knowing she was treading on thin ice.

Santa turned his head to the back of the sleigh, looking at her. "Don't the parents, what?"

"I'm just saying-- now I don't speak for all of us humans," she put her hands up in defense. "but we on Earth at a certain age believe that our parents are the ones who wrap the presents and put them under the tree." She glanced everywhere-- except at the cherry nosed faces that were glued on her. "What?" she turned over her palms and lifted them in a shrug. "It's true."

"That's preposterous, " Santa blubbered on. "I have the chimney marks to prove it!"

"You don't believe that, do you Melody?" Sam asked her.

"No... well not anymore." she glanced at his lips then back to his eyes. "You're very real to me."

"Back to what I was saying," Santa interrupted for the third time that night, "We have to hurry to make it in time for the morning." He beckoned to the sunrise that was creeping up past the horizon as dusk faded.

"Right!" Sam agreed.

"We have two sleighs that means..." Melody piped up. "We could also use the one back on the rooftop with the other reindeer. But..." she bit her lip in uncertainty. "It's all the way back there," she jutted her thumb behind her, "past London and Paris."

"If I bring you guys back there," Santa questioned, "will you able to take care of delivering presents on that side of the world?"

Both Melody and Sam stared at each other before nodding.

———

"Playing matchmaker, are we St. Nick?" Melody chuckled as she hopped out of the sleigh and onto the rooftop.

"Nope," he winked. "I'm just granting your wish. You do remember what you wished for, don't you?"

Santa, not discreetly I might add, winked at Sam who was busy with the reindeer, which caused Melody to wish she could curl up in a corner and hide.

"Santa," she stomped her feet. "You weren't supposed to say anything!"

"What?" he nonchalantly shrugged then lowered his voice so the homeowners wouldn't hear them. "I didn't do anything. It was you who wished to kiss Sam under the mi--" he quickly covered his mouth.

"Santa!" she whined and reddened as the seconds ticked by.

"Right!" he shook the reigns to let the reindeer know it was time to fly. "I best be going. On Dasher, Dancer, Prancer, Rudolph, Comet!" (The rest of the reindeer were with Melody and Sam).

Sam sauntered over to her with a cocky grin from one corner of his mouth to the other.

"Don't look at me like that," Melody commanded.

Sam's smile wasn't dimming anytime soon as he replied, "You wished for me?"

Melody snorted as she pushed him away. "That was lost in translation." She cocked her head to the side, seeing if he was buying it. "What I actually said...was...that I wanted a snack...?" Yeah, that's it! That's a pretty good lie if I do say so myself, she thought.Now she was really trying to prove it to herself. The uncertainty in her voice didn't help her one bit.

Sam still wasn't convinced. "You wished for a snack? " He weighed the two words. "Snack, Sam? Snack, Sam? That's quite a stretch even for you. They don't even sound the same. Are you sure?"

She nodded.

"So you're telling me that you wished for a snack..."

She repeated her previous actions.

"...to kiss under the mistletoe?"

She clapped her hands. "You got it! For a second you had me worried there," she leaned against Blitzen.

Sam went closer to her causing her brain to stop functioning normally. Blitzen wanting to stir up trouble, shook his brown coat and moved a few inches to the left.

She put her hands behind her to catch herself but...

A little special someone caught her before that could happen. His long eyelashes fluttered as he felt her in his arms. "You must love all things sweet, no wonder you work in a bakery."

"Uh huh," she was still stunned by how fast he had gotten to her. She could only mumble a few words.

"And it's no wonder you like me, I'm as sweet as the cherry pie you guys sell."

"Yeah. Wait, what?" She got up as soon as he said this. "You tricked me!"

Sam dismissed her defense. "I didn't trick you. Your heart did."

"Stupid heart," she muttered, staring at the rooftop shingles.

"Yeah, well mine is playing tricks on me right now," he ruffled through a regular, old, non-magical bag and pulled out the donuts that Merry had given him.

"What are you talking about?" she breathed white clouds into the air.

"Right now it's telling me that I want to kiss you," he replied.

"Oh," she said. "And what do you want to do?"

"The same thing," he shrugged as he leaned in closer.

"Wait," she eased him back just a little.

"What's wrong?"

"My wish was to kiss you under the mistletoe. Looks like it didn't come true," she playfully grinned as she teased him.

A jingling of bells was heard and a small patch of mistletoe tied in a red bow appeared falling from the sky. Well, It didn't exactly appear out of thin air, it was dropped rather.

Santa could be heard saying, "Ho, ho, ho," and flying off into the distance.

"He always comes through doesn't he?" she asked Sam.

Sam grinned. "Yeah, he does." Thanks dad.

"So what say you, Melody of this Earth?" Sam bowed as if he were her knight in shining armor.

She giggled as she took his hand and drew him closer. "Your dad, he reminds me of someone I know."

"Who?" Confusion creased across Sam's forehead.

"You, you goof!" she laughed. "Now kiss me before my lips get cold."

Placing the mistletoe, above both of their heads, he brought his lips down to hers. Tingles radiated throughout their cores and a sense of comfort rang out around them as Melody deepened the kiss.

Sam could feel the sparks fly throughout his body as his lips melted into hers.

This has been the best christmas ever.

They gazed into each other's eyes, deeply entranced and invested in one another.

"Do you still hate Christmas?" Melody asked, toying with the red scarf around his neck.

To which he replied, "Not anymore. I've found my Christmas Wish."

"That was so corny," she laughed. "How long have you been sitting on that one?"

"Cocky, are we Melody?"

She only answered him with another chuckle.

"I guess... I'll have to eat these powdered donuts by myself," he shook the bag, enticing her even more.

"That's not fair!" she said as he brought the donut closer to his mouth. "I at least have to get one-- I made them!"

"Did you now?" he loved getting a rise out of her. It was one of the things he loved most-- besides kissing her.

"Yes," she replied swiping the bag from his hands and quickly popped one into her mouth.

"Give that back," he motioned with his fingers.

"And what if I don't?"

"Melody Winona Wilson! Give that back!"

She stopped in her tracks and turned around. "How'd you know my full name?"

"I peeked at the list. Now give it here, Little Miss Christmas."

"Little Miss Christmas, I think I'm finally warming up to that."

Now it was his turn to blush. "Thanks," he sheepishly rubbed the back of his neck. "Now what say we share the donuts and head out?" he held out his hand waiting for her to take it.

He was pleasantly surprised when he felt a kiss on his cheek.

"Now let's go bring joy to the world." Melody kissed him once more as they returned to their sleigh.

How'd you guys like this chapter?

Comments, Questions?

Luckily for you readers this is not the last chapter. I repeat, this is NOT the LAST chapter. I couldn't leave you guys hanging like that.

As always thanks for reading!

Last Christmas I Gave You My Heart

Two Years Later...

"Back again so soon Little Miss Christmas?" Sam kissed her on her lips as she walked through the doors of his parents' home.

"Oh magical boy, you never cease to amaze me," she leaned down, petting the small litter of puppies that began to yap.

"How was Christmas this year?" he wondered scooping one pup into his arms.

"Tiring, I don't know how your dad did it," she rested on the carpet.

"This one reminds me of Aster." Using his index finger, he stroked the tiny puppy's white-as-snow coat.

As if on cue, the new father to be came trotting into the room.

"Hey Aster," Sam petted the older husky's head lightly. "Long time no see."

"You saw him this morning, and at lunch and now! What more could you want?" Melody asked. "You're an on-call Veterinarian!

Your job is literally seeing animals the entire day," she took one of the pups that lay on the carpet, crossed her legs and began nuzzling it.

"Yeah, but my job doesn't even hold a candle to yours," he replied gazing longingly over at her.

"Aww, I'm glad you noticed," she basked in his compliment. Her job was no walk in the park-- literally.

"How does it feel actually being Little Miss Christmas? You know my dad was right when he handed over the job to you. He saw something special in you-- something that I'm lucky to see in you everyday."

"And what is that something?" she focused her attention on the magical love of her life.

"The kindness of your heart," he touched her hand. "Being Santa Claus or at least Little Miss Christmas," he chuckled, "starts with kindness and peace and the ability to go after whatever it is that you want."

"Really? I didn't know that," she lay back with the puppy now crawling on her stomach. She laughed at how ticklish she was.

"Of course you didn't because you already had one, so I guess it came naturally to you."

"You know what also came naturally to me?" she looked over to where he sat, ugly Christmas sweater and all.

"You."

"Me?" Sam put down the pup and let it roam.

"Yeah. You," she repeated. "If you hadn't tumbled over me at the Christmas Market none of this-- you living out your dream of being a Veterinarian and me being the first woman Santa Claus, would have never happened."

Soon her pup crawled off of her and onto the spread out carpet covered in various patterns.

"I just realized something Sam," she sat up.

"And what would that be, Cutie?" he said allowing her cheeks to flourish bright red.

She chortled. "If I'm the new Mr. Claus, does that mean that you are now the Mrs. Claus and that you have to bake me cookies?"

He threw a pillow at her which she dodged. "Maybe...but only if you want me to."

"You? In an apron, I would love to see that!" she rolled on the floor laughing. "But we both know that I'm the only one with baking skills, right Sammy?"

"You are so lucky that you're the only one allowed to call me that and besides I've been known to whip up some mean brownies. Just you wait Mel."

She couldn't contain her laughter as her father-in-law-to-be held his stomach as tears pooled into his eyes from laughing so hard. "If by mean, you mean causing everyone in this house to throw up the entire night, then sure."

"I'm a good baker!" Sam protested.

"Keep telling yourself that," his mother appeared handing everyone cookies.

"Whatever helps you sleep at night," Melody munched, and for once she was happy that the cookies were chocolate chip instead of sugar cookies. She had had enough sugar cookies to last her until next Christmas.

"You."

"What?"

"You heard me," Sam grinned slyly. "You help me sleep at night or... at least keep me up," he chuckled. "Don't you remember?"

The pillow that Sam had thrown, ended up covering Melody's face as she was very red at the moment.

Why did he have to say such cringeworthy things in front of his parents?

"Oh grow up Sam," his mother hit him as he chuckled.

"So Melody," Mrs. Claus spoke to her future daughter-in-law. "What are you planning to do next, besides marry this goofball?"

Melody placed her hands in her lap, her heart heavy with love for all of these wonderful people. "We have all of our lives to get married--maybe three years from now to do so. Besides, on the days that aren't Christmas, I'll still be at Merry's Bakery, doing my day job. Merry's is like a second home to me, other than this place."

"Not only is she smart but she's also beautiful too," Sam admired the woman who could do everything and anything she wanted to. In fact, she was the one who inspired him to confess to his father that he enjoyed being a Veterinarian instead of Santa Claus. He couldn't imagine life without her.

While she lay on her back, he hovered over her so that they were both looking up at each other, but the way he hovered, her face looked as though she was upside down and vice versa. "I love you."

"I love you too Sam," she yawned.

"Looks like someone's all tired out from delivering presents tonight," he sighed at how adorable she looked even though she was extremely tired.

"No," she denied. "I'm just resting my eyes," he watched as her eyelids fluttered, sometimes for a second, sometimes they remained closed for five.

He lowered his forehead and they instantly touched. But just as he was about to lean in...

Her eyes opened slightly. "Sleep can wait. I have something better planned."

"Me too," Sam grinned playfully.

"My plan is more romantic."

"Are you sure because--"

She rolled over to the next side, got up and said, "Race you to Paris!"

"On what? A sleigh?" he asked intrigued and surprised by her proposition.

"Of course! What else?" she grabbed her coat and headed out the door into the wintry snow and Sam chasing behind her.

"Did I ever tell you how much I love those two together?" Mrs. Claus spoke to her husband as they remained by their fireplace.

"All the time dear," he smiled as he squeezed her hand and kissed it.

Sam hopped into the red sleigh and Melody hopped in the purple one.

"Hey that's no fair!" Melody called over to him as she buckled her reindeer.

"What's not fair, love?" Sam asked her as he did the same.

"That sleigh," she pointed to the one that Sam had picked, "it just got a tuneup!"

"Is that so?" Sam innocently smirked as he knew that for a fact.

"Yes," she said. "That was the sleigh I used to deliver the presents tonight. You know this," she pouted.

"What do you say, switch?"

"No," she answered.

Now he was feeling a bit skeptical. Why all of a sudden did she not want to switch?

"Why not Little Miss Christmas?" Sam caught a suspicious and dare he say it, a seductive glint in her eye.

"Because Magical boy... I just wanted to let you know that if you're going to use that sleigh, you should know that it's running low on gas!"

"Luckily I have luck on my side," he told her from the other side of the stables.

"Good luck with that," she laughed as the sleigh lifted up and floated above him.

"I also have you."

"Flattery will get you nowhere, in fact-- if my hunch is correct I should be reaching Paris in about I don't know"-- she checked her watch-- "before you."

"Sweetie don't get ahead of yourself just yet." he started up the engine but it only sputtered.

"Fine," she rolled her eyes but behind the eye rolling was a sympathetic gaze. "I'll wait until you get a full tank and then we'll race fair and square."

"You mean it?"

"Yeah, would I lie to you?"

"Let's go inside while we wait for the sleighs to fill up," his hand rested on her shoulder as they walked from the stables into the house.

"Hey, you're not trying to distract me from the race, are you?" she stopped walking.

"Not at all, Mel. You're too smart for that. Besides, I want to hear all about how Merry's Bakery is doing."

"You're serious?" she crinkled her eyebrows.

"As serious as my love for you."

"Wow, two years later and you're still so corny!" she gasped.

"Very funny. Laugh it up Mel."

She could no longer hold in her fit of chuckles anymore.

"Are you done now?" he checked his imaginary watch whereas she was wearing a real one.

"Yes," After a couple more giggles, she was able to control herself.

After going inside, away from the cold of the North Pole, they sat down by the fireplace.

"So how's Merry doing?" Sam passed Melody a steaming cup of hot chocolate. He was so busy as business picked up at Paws Veterinarian Clinic, that he could barely stop at the bakery even for two minutes.

"Wonderful actually," Melody sipped. "She got an early Christmas present courtesy of Cupid and I," she giggled, bringing the mug to her mouth once more.

"What did you do?" Sam drank his hot chocolate until it was finished and got up to get another beverage.

"With a little help...I was able to finally push those lovebirds together."

"You mean she's with Cupid?"

"No silly! Gosh you're so darn cute it hurts," she pinched one of his cheeks. "I got Mr. Mulconey and Merry together."

"Yes!" he clapped his hands.

"Why are you so happy?" she wondered.

"Because now that their love is out in the open, no more donut runs. He can just walk over and get them himself." He mixed himself a French Vanilla craving the delicious drink, and returned to her sitting on a pillow.

"But then I won't get a chance to see you," she took another sip. "With your business booming it'll be hard to catch a break."

"I'll always make time for you Melody."

Emotions rang high as romance was in the air-- or rather room. Both of their lips met and it was pure bliss.

"Really?"

"Of course Melody."

"I love you, Magical boy," she leaned in closer next to him as his arm wrapped around her waist.

"I love you too, Little Miss Christmas."

CPSIA information can be obtained
at www.ICGtesting.com
Printed in the USA
LVHW040011061222
734629LV00025B/1265

9 781837 613267